# THE WORLD OF CUSTOM TRUCKS

*Spectacular working show trucks from Europe and North America*

FERDY DE MARTIN — XAVIER STÉFANIAK

Old Pond
PUBLISHING LTD

**Ferdy De Martin**

An HGV mechanic by training, Ferdy spent more than ten years trucking across Europe, heading as far afield as the gates of Asia and the Sahara. He then worked for a humanitarian organisation, carrying out missions in several countries at war in East Africa. Ferdy now works as an engineer for a multinational. Since 1999, he has run www.TOPRUN.ch, one of the most popular internet truck sites.

**Xavier Stéfaniak**

A passion for design drew Xavier Stéfaniak to the world of custom trucks in the early 1980s. Inspired by his mentors, Francis Reyes and Patrick Pawluk, he works hard to produce the best possible art photographs of these massive beasts of the road. Originally a graphic artist/decorator, he now divides his time between his work as a truck driver in Paris and his passion. For the last seven years he has worked with several truck magazines and calendars in Europe

ISBN 978-1-908397-64-5

A catalogue record for this book is available from the British Library

Published by
Old Pond Publishing Ltd
Dencora Business Centre
36 White House Road
Ipswich IP1 5LT
United Kingdom

**www.oldpond.com**

English text translated from the French by Paul Henderson
Cover design by Ferdy De Martin and book layout by Liz Whatling
Printed and bound in China

# Contents

# Around the World

Although we have deliberately chosen to dedicate this book entirely to vehicles that travel the roads of North America and Europe, this doesn't mean that the rest of the world is devoid of trucks worthy of inclusion. Quite the contrary, as the following whistle-stop tour of the globe so vividly shows.

One of the first examples comes from Japan, where some custom trucks are completely over the top. Known as 'Dekotora', these trucks can be seen as modern Samurai whose constantly changing style is inspired by 1970s cult films and soldier figurines.

In Pakistan and Afghanistan decorated trucks have become a real cult and their drivers are kings of the road who almost have the right of life and death. Their vehicles are called 'Jingle Trucks' because they are decked with thousands of little bells.

In South America, particularly Brazil, locally assembled European-brand trucks are customised to look sporty, or even frankly aggressive. By jacking up the rear suspension as high as possible they are made to look like big cats ready to pounce!

Customising in Australia and New Zealand is more restrained, with great care being lavished on their chrome and stainless steel accessories. Stripe-based colour schemes are embellished with pin-striping motifs, applied freehand using a fine brush.

But let's get back to the book's main subject: the USA, Canada and Europe.

——— • ———

## USA et Europe : Uniquement ?

Cet ouvrage est volontairement dédié aux véhicules rencontrés sur les routes d'Amérique du Nord et d'Europe. Cela ne veut pas dire que dans d'autres parties du monde des camions dignes de figurer dans ce livre ne roulent pas, bien au contraire et pour le prouver, la page suivante nous emporte dans un rapide tour du globe !

Un des premiers exemples provient du Japon. On y trouve des camions totalement extravagants appelés "Dekotora", sorte de Samouraï moderne. Leur style, en constante évolution, est issu d'un film culte des années 70 et de figurines de guerre.

Au Pakistan et en Afghanistan, on voue une véritable adoration aux camions décorés. Leurs chauffeurs sont considérés comme les seigneurs de la route et ont presque le droit de vie ou de mort sur leurs aides chauffeurs. Ces camions sont appelés "Jingle Truck", car ils sont affublés de milliers de petites clochettes.

En Amérique du Sud, plus particulièrement au Brésil, les camions de marques Européennes, assemblés sur place, sont transformés pour adopter un look sportif voire même franchement agressif. Les suspensions arrière sont développées au maximum donnant à l'ensemble l'impression d'un félin prêt à bondir !

En Australie et en Nouvelle-Zélande, les transformations restent sobres. On soigne particulièrement les chromes et les inox ; les peintures, réalisées avec des lignes, sont enrichies avec du "Pin stripping" et effectuées au pinceau fin et à main levée.

Revenons au sujet principal de ce livre ; les USA, Canada et L'Europe

*Afghanistan.* (Photo Marcel van der Geugten)

*Japan.* (Photo Roger Snider)

*Brazil.* (Photo FB)

*New Zealand.* (Photo Simon Teahan)

# Some History

Do we know when the art of truck decoration first began?

Who first had the idea of modifying his truck to make it more beautiful, noisy and impressive, rather than improving its practicality or performance? And who, one day, decided to customise his truck just for personal satisfaction or to arouse admiration?

There's no way of answering these questions, but let's imagine a possible scenario. It's the 1950s. Twenty trucks are lined up in a parking lot. They have been there for hours, waiting for the despatch manager to come out of his office and give them a load to take to a town hundreds of kilometres away.

What is the best way to get noticed? Ensure your truck is impeccably clean? Yes, of course, but everyone has been polishing their bodywork during the wait. Leave your headlights on? Not good for the battery!

So, the only way is to be shinier and more colourful than the rest by having a wider bumper, bigger headlights, etc. Show some imagination. Stand out from the crowd.

The years go by and each country develops its own style. In northern Europe, trucks remain conservative. They are carefully painted in two or three colours, with each area sharply demarcated by stripes on the bodywork. Trucks in Great Britain are painted in family colours. Tartans are faithfully reproduced on doors, and every item in the cabin, or even the chassis, is surrounded by narrow, brush-painted borders. Southern Europeans prefer bright colours and the insides of their windscreens are decorated with all sorts of objects, the shinier the better.

By the end of the 1960s, road haulage had become international but trucks remained distinctive. When barrelling along European motorways it was easy to recognise, even from afar, an English Foden with its fairing emblazoned with the company name, followed by a Danish Scania with its light box on the roof and a Spanish Pegaso, pained in brash colours.

Then, at the beginning of the 21st century, everything was rationalised; the only thing that counted was profitability. Multinational companies took over small truck makers and standardised the styles of their vehicles. It was no longer possible to differentiate at a glance an Irish truck from a Portuguese one. The need to be different became even stronger and this was undoubtedly one of the main factors behind today's truck customising.

This is why small trucking companies are prepared to spend large amounts of their profits paying skilled craftsmen to fit luxurious upholstery and commissioning talented artists to paint unique frescoes. With much less money to spend, many independent drivers do a lot of the work themselves, spending almost all their free time customising the bodywork or interiors of their trucks. Drivers have to learn the skills of upholsterers, locksmiths and electricians.

But there is one word that applies to them all: Passion!

— • —

### Est-il possible de déterminer un commencement ?

Qui a eu le premier l'idée de modifier son camion afin qu'il soit, non pas plus pratique ou plus performant, mais plus beau, plus impressionnant, voir même plus bruyant ?! Et qui a eu, un jour, l'envie de le faire, juste pour son plaisir ou alors pour susciter de l'admiration ?

La page de droite illustre de façon beaucoup trop succincte, car ce n'est pas le sujet de livre, quelques exemples de camions qui se sont distingués dans les rassemblements de camions des années 70 – 80.

*Jean-Marie's Scania is the best-decorated and most customised truck at the 1982 Le Mans 24 Hours.*

*An early 1990s Saurer D330 with a carefully executed paint job and a truly massive bull bar. (Photo Michel Bezencon)*

*Californian company Canepa customises trucks to make them more aerodynamic and spacious. (Photo Canepa Design)*

*The cabin of this early 1980s Scania has been extended, making it ideal for the driver's regular trips between Europe and Arabia. (Photo Ashley Coghill collection)*

## Peterbilt 351, Maggini & Son Trucking (USA)

The United States has two schools of old-timers. As could be expected, the first school believes in recreating identical copies of the factory model. The second school, an example of which you can see here, is not always to the taste of purists. However, spend some time looking at the photographs of this superb example of old-school style with a dash of hot-rod spirit and you will surely find it grows on you.

Strangely, the soft and elegant aspect of Maggini & Son's 1962 Peterbilt 351 is more likely to awaken the dormant beast than soothe the spirit of the connoisseur of fine trucks that you are. Its elegant, avant-garde lines and great class are brought to the fore by the paint scheme of green flames licking across a superb yellow background.

Chrome is king in the United States, and there is no shortage of it on this Maggini truck. From the front bumper to the full wheels, from the rear fenders to the exhaust stacks, from the deck cover to the visor and the numerous chrome-plated original parts, the mirror effect shimmers brightly under the blazing Californian sun. The cab is dominated by green engine-turned stainless steel and black leather. As in all self-respecting major custom jobs, freehand arabesques and lettering are legion on Maggini's Pete.

As you can see, this 351 is exceptional, in good taste and peppered with touches of originality: what more could you want?

———•———

L'esprit old school proche du mouvement « hot rod », est ici superbement mis en valeur.

Le Peterbilt 351 de 1962 est une vraie bête qui sommeille. Sa ligne avant-gardiste et élancée, se révèle au grand jour grâce aux chromes qui brillent de mille feux sous le soleil brûlant de Californie. Comme tout projet "Kustom"qui se respecte, les arabesques et lettrages sont réalisés à la main.

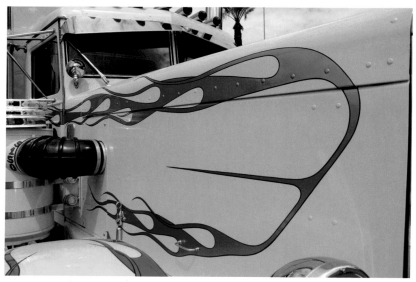

*The sprawling flames make the hood look even longer than it is.*

*The contrast between the metallic green flames and yellow background works to spectacular effect*

*A superb marriage of bright colours and chrome.*

Numerous arabesques decorate this Californian truck.

The headlights, grille and air filters are characteristic of the 351.

The company name is displayed on the rear bumper.

*The Pete's cabin has been slightly modernised.*

*The Californian sun provides the ideal backdrop for this line-up of rare Peterbilt 352 COEs.*

This rear view of the 352 shows how the rear panel of the cab has been profiled to accommodate the exhaust stacks.

## Volvo FH16 700, Dieppedalle Transports (France)

Its unusual colour – a standard tint produced by the Italian truck maker Fiat, enhanced by the addition of pearl yellow – is far from being the only attractive feature of this 700-horsepower Volvo FH. Although Eric, the truck's owner, would never call himself the greatest fan of decorated trucks, his desire to do something different and his wish to have a truck that stands out led him to embrace what is a rapidly growing movement among France's custom truck enthusiasts. This movement, which has long been comfortably installed in Scandinavia and the Netherlands, is a rich source of ideas for those who dare to go down such a road.

Scania occupies a dominant place in European truck shows, with Volvo being the only brand capable of offering any real resistance to this dominance. It has to be said that this task is made much easier by custom jobs as good as Eric's.

Delivered directly to Thierry Gremilliet of ATG Décors at St Marcel-lès-Valence in the south of France, the colours, the portraits of Eric's daughters on the back of the cab, and the Volvo 700-horsepower logos on the sides were agreed between Eric and the painter. When he picked up his FH, Eric was absolutely delighted with the result.

Ordered with full air ride, the Volvo has a superbly aggressive allure when the suspension is fully lowered. The accessories that were added, partly on the basis of Eric's drawings, magnify this effect even further, and his grille-hugging, stainless steel bull bar, fairing and roof bars are truly exceptional. Other, more conventional accessories include the exhaust stacks, the stainless steel rear bumper and the blue-painted deck cover.

Eric aimed to produce an outstanding, innovative truck, and in that he has definitely succeeded.

—— • ——

Ce Volvo siglé 700ch semble agressif avec l'air ride intégral abaissée au maximum. L'effet est accentué par les accessoires réalisés d'après les dessins d'Eric, son propriétaire. Ainsi nous pouvons découvrir pour la 1ère fois sur un camion : le pare-buffles inox qui épouse à merveille les contours des calandres, les barres de carénages et de toit, les échappements type cathédrale, le pare-chocs arrière full inox et la tôle du châssis peinte en bleue.

*The sun brings out the pearl yellow of the colour scheme.*

*Thanks to its air ride, this ground-hugging FH has really clean lines.*

*Details of the portraits that decorate the back of the Volvo's cab.*

*This project has stainless steel everywhere: fuel tank, exhausts, bumpers – nothing is left to chance.*

*Chrome may be hard to clean but it sure looks good....*

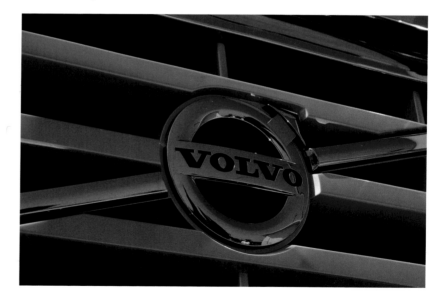

## Scania R730, Nicolo' (Italy)

For the last few years the fashion in Italy has been to decorate every part of the cab with chrome-plated steel or aluminium components. Such trucks conjure images of knights in shining armour.

However, not everyone has followed this trend. Nicolo' had his own idea of what he wanted to do with both the cab and the bodywork. For instance, the back of the truck is directly inspired by the Corvette ZR1, and the lights are incorporated into a rounded moulding that merges perfectly into the lines of the skirts.

Using slender Peugeot 206 headlamps was a very spectacular and unique way of giving a racy elegance to the roof fairing. The interior is luxuriously upholstered in white and purple leather, and illuminated by LEDs that automatically change colour.

'Il Viola', as Nicolo' calls it, has won top prizes at every meeting it has taken part in; meetings he fits in to the truck's round of refrigerated transport deliveries between Italy and northern Europe.

It is not only custom truck enthusiasts who find the Nicolo' impressive; it also appeals to women, who love its mauve-and-violet colour scheme.

———•———

Nicolo' n'a pas succombé à la tendance de couvrir son camion de chrome et d'inox comme c'est la mode en Italie. Il a privilégié les modifications d'éléments de la cabine et du carénage. L'arrière, inspiré de la Corvette ZR1, et l'intégration spectaculaire et inédite de phares avant de Peugeot, donnent une élégance racée au véhicule. L'intérieur est luxueusement capitonné avec un cuir blanc et mauve surpiqué de LED colorées.

"Il viola", comme le surnomme son chauffeur, a raflé les plus hautes distinctions dans chaque meeting où il s'est présenté en Italie et dans le nord de L'Europe.

*At its first meeting outside Italy, Nicolo' won the top prize for trucks at the Le Mans 24 Hours in 2011.*

*A giant Griffin on a pearly background gives the truck a unique personality.*

A dazzling array of lights runs from the chassis to the roof.

Changes in the colour of the interior lights are automatic and programmable.

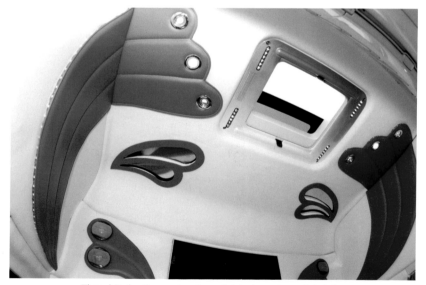

The white leather makes the cab interior extremely bright.

*In Italy, organisers of truck meetings like to invite pretty girls, who are always willing to pose for photographers.*

## International Lonestar, 'Bad Habit' (USA)

It is extremely difficult to produce a truly extraordinary truck that stands out from the crowd. One of the few people to manage this feat is New Jersey International dealer Jason Carello, who has used the characteristic shape of the Lonestar to great advantage.

Although few external modifications have been made, a small number of parts have been added to embellish the IH. For those who are new to the International brand, here are some of the most artful additions: an open grille; a stainless-steel strip to lower the original bumpers; a pointed Kustom sun visor; wider exhausts; ever-fashionable Cool Components rear fenders; smooth cab walls; deck covers on and below the chassis, which has been extended by 120 cm, and new rear bumpers. The air ride gives the truck a blacktop-hugging profile.

As in any self-respecting project, the customising would not be complete without a paint scheme worthy of the name. ETC are masters of this type of high-precision work and, it has to be said, they have truly done themselves proud with 'Bad Habit', as the flawless candy-red gloss perfectly sets off the Lonestar's curves and corners.

According to Jason it was too 'bland' on its own, so swathes of cream edged with grey shadows were added to spice up the International's look.

— • —

Avec une peinture Candy polie lustrée, soigneusement projetée et au rendu sublime, incluant des incrustations de bandes en mouvement de couleur crème rehaussées d'une ombre grise, voici l'International Lonestar. Ce camion US est le plus moderne du marché avec un style custom classique comportant des retouches bien vues, comme par exemple la calandre ajourée, une visière custom pointue, des échappements plus gros et un châssis allongé de 1m20. Une vraie réussite.

*The air filter is a marvel in its own right.*

The Lonestar is very contemporary, as are the accessories and modifications.

*Combining candy-red with swathes of cream gives a superb result.*

*Extended fenders, chrome in profusion, and custom-built wheels – truly faultless.*

## Volvo FH16 600, Ronny Ceusters Transport (Belgium)

The arrival of a new Ronny Ceusters at European meetings is a mouth-watering event for many enthusiasts, and this new FH, destined for Peter Van Loon, is no exception. First seen at the Assen Truck Festival in 2011, the famous Belgian company's 600-horsepower Volvo Globetrotter left many of the make's aficionados speechless.

So let's take a closer look at the FH. With a classic 6 x 2 configuration, the Volvo has the minimum amount of accessories. In addition to the original Volvo array Ronny has added clearance lights and air horns to the roof, lights below the mirrors and on the skirts, and marker lights below the front bumpers. The rear of the truck has been fitted with square tail lights and a chequer-plate frame tail. Finally, custom-made fairings have been added to replace the original models. Nothing else was needed to produce a fabulous result.

Once again, this FH uses the sober and classy colours that have become the hallmark of Ceusters' trucks and a sure bet in the world of custom trucks. Borrowed from a Danish transporter, the bronze, red, white and grey are astutely arranged for optimal effect. Frescoes of Vikings on either side of the raised cab roof give an additional personal touch.

The rear box bears a US-inspired pin-striping motif, a radical touch that sets the tone for this FH – hug the ground, as low as possible. Superb!

———•———

Lorsqu'un "Ronny Ceusters" pointe son nez sur les expos continentales, il fait saliver bon nombre de passionnés. D'une configuration classique ce Volvo propose le « minimum » pour ce qui est des accessoires. Il faut préciser qu'il n'en faut pas plus pour un tel rendu.

Ses couleurs qui sont devenues mythiques (bronze, rouge, blanche et grise) sont astucieusement disposées pour un rendu optimal. La touche personnelle apparaît sous la forme d'une décoration figurative, représentant des vikings.

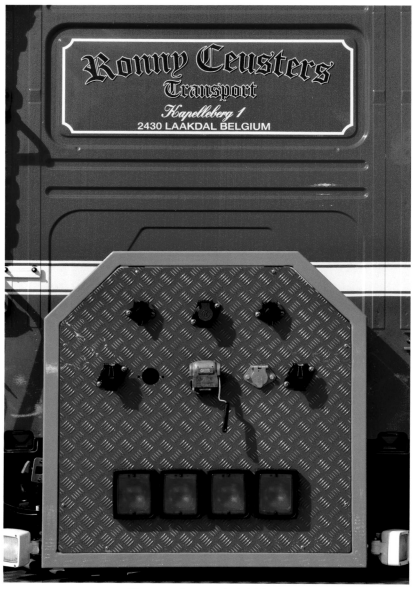

*The connectors are nicely laid out.*

*Twinned styles, contemporary and traditional: the alchemy works.*

*The paintwork is a mixture of airbrushing, pin-striping and stripes.*

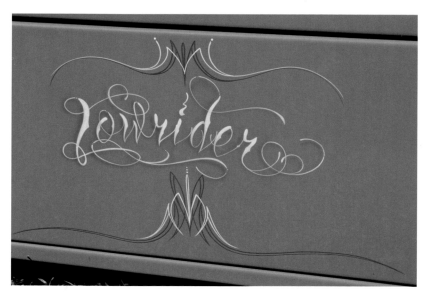

*The Danish interior with its velour and white leather is wonderfully cosy.*

## Scania R620, 'Jo Siffert', Müller (Switzerland)

Müller is a family firm that has specialised in temperature-controlled transport for several generations. Easily recognisable thanks to their bright green paintwork, all the company's trucks are maintained in perfect condition, both mechanically and aesthetically, as can be seen at weekends, when the fleet lines up behind the family farm in central Switzerland.

Most of the fleet is made up of tractor units with refrigerated trailers, but it also includes a few triple-axle straight trucks. Müller trucks spend most of their working lives on the highways and byways of Switzerland, but they can occasionally be seen neighbouring countries, such as Italy.

Franz Müller has dedicated his Scania R620 to Jo Siffert, Switzerland's most famous racing driver, who can be seen in his 'Gulf' Porsche racing against Steve McQueen in the 1971 film *Le Mans*. One of Porsche's top drivers, Siffert resisted strenuous efforts by Ferrari to entice him to F1. He died in 1971, in a tragic accident during a commemorative race at Brands Hatch.

——— • ———

L'intérieur de la cabine est luxueusement capitonné d'une couleur uniforme, le vert de la société, ainsi que la carrosserie. L'ensemble de la décoration de ce Scania R620 est dédié au plus fameux coureur automobile suisse Jo Siffert. Pilote fétiche chez Porsche, il est fortement sollicité par Ferrari pour courir en F1. Jo décède en 1971 à Brands Hatch suite à un tragique accident lors d'une course commémorative.

*Franz Müller poses in front of the portrait of Jo Siffert.*

*Apart from some grey trim, green is the only colour used.*

*Even the sport steering wheel and dashboard are in the company green.*

*The quilted ceiling contrasts nicely with the freshness of the green paintwork.*

*The entirely redesigned rear bumper is very simple.*

*Waterproof toolboxes have replaced the side skirts.*

*An apple-green truck seen through an apple tree!*

*The portrait of Jo Siffert in shades of green perfectly matches the truck's aesthetics.*

*With its air suspension lowered, the truck looks ready to race.*

## Peterbilt 389, Farmers Oil Company Inc. (USA)

Although it is true that the vast majority of Peterbilt 359s and 379s presented during the last few years have adopted an old-school style, more recent models, painted attractive colours and adorned with stripes, are also worthy of serious attention.

Jessica and Jeremy Graves have adopted a truly judicious mix of stripes and metallic colours for their Farmers Oil Peterbilt 389. To produce their new rig the couple called upon the services of CSM in Joplin, Missouri. At first sight, few major modifications appear to have been made, as the areas that have been customised blend in perfectly with the whole. Consequently, modifying the bumpers and adding larger exhausts, a suicide sun visor and WTI fenders was all that was needed. Of course, it has the indispensable LED lights that our American friends love so much.

As the Graves' goal was to produce an old-school truck, the paint scheme was a vitally important part of the project. CSM boss Brian Martin and his team chose a metallic champagne as the main colour for the tanker and 389 red for the two chassis and for features such as the fuel tanks and the stripes, which are outlined with brown-and-yellow borders.

This combination clearly shows its retro side, aiming to maintain an external aspect similar to the original…. The Americans never stop amazing us!

———— • ————

C'est dans les ateliers C.S.M. de Joplin Missouri que sont choisis et installés les équipements "Kustom". La peinture est composée d'un champagne métal pour la teinte principale de la citerne et du 389, et d'un rouge pour les 2 châssis et divers éléments comme les réservoirs et les bandes rehaussées d'un marron surligné de jaune.

Ce combo présente clairement son côté « rétro actuel » visant à conserver un aspect extérieur proche de l'origine, … les américains n'ont pas fini de nous étonner !!

*The interior is classy and in harmony with the exterior.*

*The company name is written on the fuel tanks.*

*Stripes are coming back into fashion across the Atlantic.*

*This Peterbilt 389 trailer-tanker combination is both magnificent and unusual.*

The company name is beautifully integrated into the stripe on the back of the tanker.

The cable and hose connectors are elegantly laid out.

*Chrome for the accessories, champagne and red for the bodywork - the combination works perfectly!*

## Scania T460 Longline, J. Peeters & Zn (Belgium)

'Everything is possible' is the truck's nickname. No one would argue!

Now a collector's truck, partly because it is no longer produced but mostly because it is rare, the Scania T Longline EXC is a sure bet for every lucky owner. Bought second-hand from a Dutch transporter, the Longline shown here is a wonderful addition to Marc Peeters' personal museum in Booischot, Belgium.

The proud owner of several older Scanias, including a 1985 tanker truck in Esso livery and a 141 in 6 x 2 configuration, Peeters knows very well what the word restoration means. After passing through the hands of local bodywork experts Spiessens to be painted in the company's colours, it moved on to Diego's car repair to have the murals added. Peeters then had a luxury interior fitted by the Dutch company Special Interior.

As for every exceptional truck, winning prizes and trophies depends on incorporating a harmonious array of accessories. With this in mind, Peeters has added several bars of LEDs and a Scania logo to the raised cab, and dotted LEDs along the fairings and the bottom of the bumpers. The truck also boasts under-body boxes, a deck cover, Norwegian-style rear bumpers and American exhaust stacks. The chrome sun visor, company logo and Michelin men so dear to many Belgian projects add the final touches to this Longline.

———•———

« Everything is possible », c'est le surnom du camion, on ne lui donne pas tort !...

Camion de collection du fait de sa rareté, le Scania T topline EXC est une valeur sûre.

Il est agrémenté d'une panoplie homogène d'accessoires comme les barres leds ou logo Scania incrustés sur la rehausse, les carénages ou encore le bas du pare-chocs. Un "longline" d'une esthétique rare !

*Arabesques are very fashionable.*

46

*A mix of English and Belgian truck culture, the style works.*

*The cab is classy – you just want to get in and drive!*

*The finish on this Griffin is amazing.*

## Volvo FH16 700, 'Bruce Springsteen', Van Dalen (Netherlands)

Since it was first presented in competition three years ago, Harry Van Dalen's Volvo has been a frequent conversation piece for truck enthusiasts. What we have here is a very tasty morsel, as the style and care with which it was produced are simply staggering. Specialist airbrush painters MW Designs and Kentie Truck Specials, past masters at radical bodywork and interior transformations, have exercised every bit of their talents on this truck.

The project first passed through the hands of Kentie, who gave the FH a radical look by adding skirts to the chassis, new bumpers and fairings, exhaust stacks, a harmonious lighting array on the roof that includes blue flashing lights, and Trux bull bars. The effect of these changes was amplified by adding full air suspension. At the same time, Kentie set to work on the FH's cab, producing an impeccable interior of beige leather/Alcantara with painted violet-marble trim.

Once these two jobs had been completed, the truck went to MW Designs for painting. Harry, a music fan in his spare time, chose a musical theme in the shape of Bruce Springsteen, alias The Boss. Painted using the tone-on-tone technique and combined with silver tribal arrows, the result is perfect.

Nothing has been overlooked with this project.

———•———

Nous avons ici un morceau de choix, dont le style et le soin accordé à la réalisation sont tout simplement ahurissants ! MW Designs, spécialiste des réalisations à l'aérographe et Kentie Trucks Specials, maître dans les transformations radicales de carrosserie et intérieur, ont tour à tour mis en exergue leur talent sur ce Volvo FH.

Harry Van Dalen opte pour une décoration musicale dédiée à Bruce Springsteen, le « boss ». Réalisé en ton sur ton, le rendu, associé aux flèches tribales argent, est sublime.

*The theme is Bruce Springsteen, alias The Boss.*

*Violet is rarely used and therefore ideal if you want to stand out from other show trucks.*

*The silver arrows integrate perfectly with the bull bar.*

*An enormous amount of work went into the chassis.*

*It's all in the contrast: the beige interior is composed of Alcantara and leather. Note the little touches of violet marble.*

The singer's famous guitar reigns over the deck cover.

The back of the cab hasn't been forgotten; it depicts an original painting of The Boss.

## Scania R560, P Bjarne Andersen Transport (Denmark)

Customising a truck is a way to be different. But even in this 'minority' field, we are starting to see a lot of differences between projects. Individuality is shown first of all in the choice of style. Whether it is a Nordic mixture of genres, classic English old school, French airbrush murals or American extreme customising, the style chosen for a truck is often a reflection of the driver's personality.

Morten, a fan of the Swedish Griffin brand, is known and admired throughout the closed world of customised trucks, as is his Scania R560.

P Bjarne Andersen, with its red, grey and cream trucks, is one of the most prominent companies on the European show-truck circuit. In order to celebrate the company's 40th birthday, the colours and layout of the stripes have been slightly modified.

Morten's desire to give his Scania a slightly quirky look has resulted in this highly restrained Griffin with its painted hubs, pin-striping, decorative stripes and old-style accessories, such as the Michelin men and the deck cover. The interior is in tune with the rest, with pin-striping, paintwork and plush in Denmark's national colours.

There is no doubt that the fertility of creative imagination shown by customisers promises a long and happy future for atypical projects.

———•———

Morten, authentique passionné de Scania, est connu et reconnu dans ce monde « fermé » du camion "Kustom". Son R560 de l'une des compagnies européennes les plus en vue dans les Truck Beauty Contest. Les camions rouge, gris et crème de P. Bjarne Andersen sont une véritable référence tout en sobriété, avec des jantes peintes, des pinstrippings, des filets et des accessoires typés "old school".

*The principle, 'enough is enough', underpins this customising.*

*Its old-school style will ensure this Danish Scania doesn't go unnoticed.*

The Danish velvet, white leather, red paintwork and arabesques of the interior go perfectly with the Griffin's exterior.

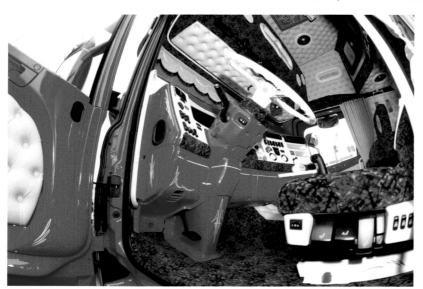

*The pure white bumpers and wheels are a wonderful match for the Scania's red-and-grey paint scheme.*

## Kenworth W900, Lanita Transport, Scott Diller (USA)

Who would have imagined that starting from an old wreck of a 1981 Kenworth W900A, Elizabeth Truck Center in Elizabeth, New Jersey, would be able to produce a modern show truck with such a great mix of contemporary and period features? Not many. But that underestimates ETC's employees, the haute couturiers of the truck world.

Let's have a look at the Ken. Four years, yes, four long years were needed to produce this exceptional W900A. Owned by Scott Diller, a haulier from Myerstown, Pennsylvania, the Kenworth closely resembles the original, which was Diller's objective. The general look of the truck was carefully thought out, as was the choice of components.

Stage One of the project was to completely strip and shot-blast the truck. Then, the cab and sleeper compartment were fully refurbished in a most befitting way. Out with the rust holes produced by being parked outside for two years; goodbye to the dented bodywork and rivets. Wishing to respect the truck's old-school look as far as possible, the glossy red-and-black paintwork provides the crowning touch to the desired retro style.

Although the additional accessories were chosen in the same sprit, only modern parts were used. As a result, the exhaust stacks, the Valley bumper and the plunging rear fenders sparkle brightly, as do the original accessories that the specialists found and refurbished as good as new.

The exterior style continues through the cab interior, which boasts a custom dashboard, painted floor and door panels, and shiny black leather upholstery.

———•———

4 longues années auront été nécessaires à la réalisation de ce Kenworth W900A issu d'une casse automobile. Il semble proche de l'origine, et c'est l'aspect recherché. Pour respecter au maximum le côté « old school », la peinture rouge et noire brillante apporte sans contestation LA touche qu'il manquait au style rétro désiré. Les filets et "pinstripping" qui courent tout le long de ce camion se retrouvent jusque dans la cabine.

*This fabulous 1981 W900A is an invitation to take to the road.*

*Four years were needed to achieve this superb finish!*

*The cab uses the same colours as the bodywork.*

The red and black contrast perfectly with the chrome.

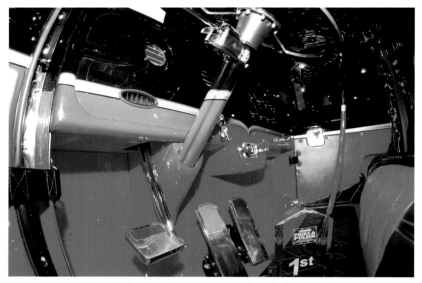

Note the bodywork stripes repeated inside the cab and the requisite pin-striping on the wall of the sleeper.

*In a word, magnificent!*

## Scania R620 EXC 'Triple X', Michel Kramer (Netherlands)

Produced in close collaboration with MW Designs and Special Interior, Michel Kramer's Scania EXC represents the pinnacle of exterior customising. Unique, original, incredible – it is all of these things and more. Although the paint scheme à la française is not the most popular style for Dutch projects, the care and attention bestowed on this Griffin make it one of the best European paint jobs of recent years.

This colossal project began with an extensive remodelling of the bodywork, including an extended sleeper, a new grille, lower suspension, smooth rear wall and chassis skirts, and a wrap-around rear bumper. And that's all it took!

Next it was the turn of the paint scheme. The choice was endless, or almost, but the decision to depict the film *Triple X* was a thunderbolt in Dutch custom truck culture, as the Dutch generally prefer stripes to murals.

Every great project has to have a matching interior, and the magicians of Special Interior have produced a fabulous shop window for their talents. Lined with leather and Alcantara, and with judicious touches of paintwork, the cab is a paragon of luxurious refinement.

With such a gem in his hands, Michel did not want to overload it with all sorts of accessories. A set of spoke rims, top and bottom light bars and a suicide sun visor do just the job.

Today, the Dutch style is a source of imagination and inspiration. You have the result in front of your eyes.

——•——

Inédit, original, incroyable… Réalisé en étroite collaboration avec MW Designs et Special Interior, le Scania EXC de Michel Kramer atteint des sommets dans la préparation custom : allongement de la profondeur de la couchette, changement de la calandre, de la paroi arrière et fermeture du châssis lisse, pare-chocs arrière enveloppant, et bien d'autres détails, un travail colossal. C'est le style hollandais qui est aujourd'hui une véritable source d'inspiration !

This Griffin is adorned with many customised parts. Can you spot them?

*Grille, skirts, bumpers and wheels make up just a tiny fraction of the modifications to this truck.*

*The wonderfully cosy interior uses the same colours as the bodywork. Magnificent.*

*The airbrushed decoration on the smooth walls is lit up at night.*

*The actor Vin Diesel stars on both sides of the truck.*

72

*Note the exhaust.*

## Peterbilt 379, 'Disorderly Conduct', Paul Voigt, CSM (USA)

Almost new! Paul Voigt's Peterbilt 379 is one of the most outstanding American projects of the last three years. Originally built in 1999, this mouth-watering truck has been completely refurbished from top to bottom. Starting from almost nothing, CSM has produced a complete restoration, halfway between old school and modernity. Here's how....

Only after completely stripping the vehicle and shot-blasting the chassis could the changes begin. Although it looks similar to the original, the truck has undergone numerous modifications. The most obvious changes include the extended chassis, the drooped fenders on both the cab and refrigerated trailer, and the chrome parts, such as the exhausts, the bumper and the suicide sun visor.

Other changes are less ostentatious. The most striking features are probably the transparent rear bulkheads on the fuel tanks, which show the diesel inside and, as a real show-stopper, light up at night! Other highlights include: the electric-blue and gloss-black paintwork with the sponsors' names painted tone-on-tone on a blue background; the painted or chromed innards, and the underside of the trailer.

The cab has also been given the top-of-the-range treatment needed to stand out from the competition, with a 359 dashboard, mahogany floor and interior trim, and cream leather for the rest.

A lot of people will be very envious of this truck, there's no doubt about that.

———•———

CSM signe ici une restauration complète à mi-chemin entre old-school et modernité. Explications : allongement du châssis, ailes tombantes, des éléments chromés comme les tubes d'échappement, le bumper et la visière suicide. L'intérieur de la cabine est en acajou et cuir beige. Et le plus marquant : des réservoirs diesel transparents avec un lightshow incorporé.

*The truck's name is written on the trailer.*

*Hats off to the talented team at CSM for this sculptural project.*

Some of the innovative modifications to this 379 combo.

*Lighting is an essential part of major projects in the United States.*

*The leather, wood, paintwork and embroidery go perfectly with the blue lighting. The paint scheme makes the bonnet look even longer than it is.*

*One of the most extraordinary and accomplished projects of recent years. Well done, Paul!*

## Volvo F1220 Globetrotter, Reto Lendenmann (Switzerland)

Presented at Geneva Truck Show in 1979, the new Volvo F12 Globetrotter immediately attracted the crowds. In fact, it was the first production cab in which the driver could stand upright. Reto Lendenmann bought this truck in 1996, since when he has never stopped working on it and improving it, despite continuing to use it for international haulage work.

He fitted out the cab himself, incorporating some novel ideas and greatly improving its comfort. His numerous innovations include a 120-cm-wide bed, a second single bed, retractable seats and a washbasin with tap. Reto wanted to keep the colour of the cab exactly the same as when it was presented in Geneva, a series of blues that are part and parcel of the Globetrotter legend.

The truck is now almost retired but it is still in perfect condition. It will soon be converted into a leisure vehicle – it already has a bicycle rack behind the cab and an electric generator is about to be installed in the chassis.

—— • ——

Depuis 1996, Reto n'a jamais cessé de réviser et d'améliorer ce "Globe", malgré les transports internationaux qu'il effectuait avec.

Il a lui-même aménagé la cabine avec des idées inédites améliorant le confort, comme par exemple un vrai grand lit de 120 cm de large, un deuxième de 85 cm, des sièges escamotables et même un lavabo. Il a conservé les couleurs de la cabine, une série de bleus dégradés, qui ont rendu le Globe-trotter si mythique.

*The chassis is completely covered with aluminium chequer-plate panels that cleverly hide the cables and air hoses.*

*Coupled to a stainless-steel tanker, Reto's Globetrotter looks stunning.*

Reto fitted out the cab himself, adding a lot of storage space. The Volvo logo is printed on the bottom of the large foldaway bed.
A washbasin with tap is integrated into the dashboard, and the box between the seats will hold a lot more than an iPad!

*Additions to the truck are of very high quality; the result is restrained and very modern.*

*Reto made his own customised system to fit the US-style exhaust stacks
and to hide the trailer cable.*

*Reto's Volvo looks newer than new, despite being twenty years old.*

## Mercedes MP4, 'Xtar', Kuljetus Auvinen Oy, (Finland)

In 2001 Mika Auvinen began presenting a brand-new Mercedes Actros every year. Each successive truck was increasingly customised and seemed to attain new heights of sophistication.

In 2006, Mika dropped the Mercedes star for the Scania Griffin and its new R-series cab. This gave rise to two 25.5 m monsters, 'Shogun' and 'Gunfighter', which swept the board at Scandinavian competitions.

In 2011, Mika was once again seduced by the 3-pointed star, whose new cab convinced him to return to the Mercedes fold. He dreamed up the warrior 'Xtar', who became the main character in the murals that cover every side of the vehicle.

———•——

Depuis 2001, Mika Auvinen avait pour habitude de nous présenter chaque année un camion toujours plus "customisé" qui semblait à chaque fois atteindre les limites de la sophistication, des monstres de 25,5 mètres de long, "Shogun et Gunfighter" et qui raflaient tous les prix.

En 2011 Mika est séduit par la nouvelle cabine de Mercedes et décide d'en faire son nouveau camion fétiche. La guerrière Xtar nait de son imagination et devient le personnage principal que l'on voit évoluer sur des fresques gigantesques tout autour du véhicule.

*The beautiful 'Xtar' was dreamed up by the truck's owner.*

The cold, interlaced colours are particularly suited to the angles of the Mercedes MP4's cab.

Mika Auvinen has been a leading light in truck customising for over ten years.

Verhoomo Prima's interior is reminiscent of the 1960s futurist style often depicted in graphic novels.

Xtar, the warrior, covers the back of the trailer.

A beauty from space come to save planet earth.

*Hundreds of LEDs cover just about every component, including the tanker reinforcement, which is adorned with red mini-LEDs.*

The new Mercedes cab is ultra practical. It even has a sofa
so the driver can relax in comfort

Xtar's fenders protect the wheels on the combo's seven axles.

The hydraulic pistons used to empty the tanker are hidden under a chrome pillar
bearing the 3-pointed Mercedes star

Come from another planet, the warrior Xtar does not need to fight too hard to carry off the top prizes at truck shows.

## Scania R580 Topline, Fred Greenwood & Son (UK)

Transporting live animals is a delicate business that requires a lot of experience and respect for both the animals and current legislation. The Greenwood family has three generations of expertise in this field. Based in Yorkshire, in the centre of England, their red-and-cream trucks travel the length and breadth of the United Kingdom.

Although their deliveries are to large industrial complexes, they have to pick up their loads in the middle of the countryside, so Jo, the driver of the R580, often has to drive long distances along narrow roads lined with overhanging branches, and then negotiate rough farm tracks between dry-stone walls. These minor roads are much prettier than the motorways but they are very stressful for the driver, who has to be constantly on his guard, as a single branch can destroy hours of painstaking brushwork.

With their resolutely British style, Greenwood's trucks have an old-school look that perfectly suits the countryside through which they are driven.

———— • ————

Par leur style résolument "British" les camions Greenwood ont un look "Old school" qui s'associe agréablement avec le paysage dans lequel ils évoluent.

Si les lieux de livraison sont de grands complexes industriels, il n'en est pas de même pour les lieux de chargement. Jo, le chauffeur du R730, doit régulièrement emprunter d'étroites routes bordées d'arbres aux branches trop basses, avant de s'enfiler dans des chemins privés aux murs de pierres saillantes menant chez les éleveurs. Une conduite qui demande une attention sans faille.

*Jo decided to mix British and Nordic styles by placing a 'Swedish' bull bar over the grille and adding a 'Danish' box to the top of the cab,*

*Greenwood's eye-catching cattle truck stands out on the narrow roads of the Yorkshire Dales National Park.*

Two of the company's Scanias have been faithfully airbrushed onto the underside of the top bunk.

The cab upholstery uses exactly the same colours as the bodywork.

Each section of the cab is outlined in typically British style.

In its 6 x 2 version, with a lateral exhaust, the truck has a very harmonious look.

*Great care has been taken with the whole vehicle. The numerous hand-painted stripes give this Scania a touch of class.*

## Peterbilt 379, Jade Transport Ltd (Canada)

Since the time of Copernicus, we have known that the earth revolves around the sun. Some trucks have the same aura, not just for their colour but also for their general attractiveness. With this Peterbilt 379, Jonathan Robert Dyck has produced a truck that is both out-of-the-ordinary and classic. A fan of US truck customising since Shift Products was founded, Jonathan wanted to show off his skills through this 379.

Let's start at the front. The originality of the bumpers, made from two parts joined together, immediately leaps out. This sets the tone for the rest of the modifications: a convex grille with thin slats, state-of-the-art LED headlights and personalised wing-mirror arms.

The sides of the truck dance to the same tune, with fibreglass step plates that extend back to the fuel tanks, dual-exit exhausts under the sleeper, and six superb carbon-fibre fenders. Originally developed for competition purposes, carbon fibre was also used for the air filters (taken from a Subaru), the Racing wind deflector on top of the sleeper, the wing mirrors and the thin parts on the rear bumper. The truck's rear bumper is, in fact, an original mix of contemporary and old school.

As you can see, the competitive spirit is everywhere. In order to maintain that trend, Jonathan had his Pete painted metallic orange, to which he has added some judiciously located black stripes. Attractiveness, originality, difference … the objective has been attained!

——— • ———

Un Peterbilt de compétition. Calandre convexe à fines lamelles, phares à LED dernier cri, et bras de rétroviseurs personnalisés affutent les lignes de la cabine. Des marchepieds en fibre courant jusqu'aux réservoirs, les tubes d'échappements sous la couchette en double sortie et pour compléter la bête de course : 6 magnifiques ailes en carbone. Voici un 379 qui se place directement en "pole position"

*The combination of metallic orange and matt black suits this Canadian Peterbilt perfectly.*

*Extended chassis and air ride – the racing spirit is everywhere.*

*The carbon fibre produces an undeniable racing effect.*

*The unusual shapes give the Peterbilt a new look*

*Carbon fibre has a unique look – superb.*

*The absence of exhaust stacks is a step away from the usual North American style.*

## Scania R620, S-U-P-E-R (Switzerland)

There are only a few Swiss trucks that really make the grade in customising. The current owner, Beat, has placed a stylised S-U-P-E-R logo on top of the cab. This logo was used for the launch of the 0-series cab (Scania 140 V8) in 1969 and has since been reused by fans of 1970s trucks.

Today, the truck is permanently coupled to a trailer for transporting racing cars, and the two parts form a very harmonious and restrained whole.

———— • ————

Il n'y a que quelques camions suisses qui sont de réelles références en matière de tuning ! Ce R620 en fait incontestablement partie ! Malgré son état esthétique irréprochable, ce véhicule est déjà à la retraite. Il a effectivement plusieurs années d'intense activité dans le transport international. L'une des transformations la plus spectaculaire est la suppression des poignées de portes qui confère à la cabine une allure de voiture de sport haut de gamme.

*The bull bar is the same as those seen on many trucks in northern Scandinavia.*

*Fitted out to transport two racing cars, the trailer has a workshop, kitchen, bed and lounge.*

*Each side of the light bar bears a Flipje mascot, a character invented by a Dutch jam-maker in the 1930s. The R620 embroidered into the carpet is the engine horsepower.*

*The interior of the cabin is entirely covered in suede.*

*Something seems to be missing.... There are no door handles! A 1970s Scania logo adorns a panel on the rear wall of the cab.*

*The proof that show trucks don't go out only when it is sunny!*

## Peterbilt 379, Ryans Feed (USA)

Apart from the chrome wheels and the burgundy paintwork, at first sight this Ryans Peterbilt looks as if it belongs to the conservative school of custom trucks, rather than to the flamboyant school. Even though it has quite aggressive lines, the entire job speaks of perfectly measured aesthetic purity.

However, behind this apparent simplicity, the truck teems with carefully judged details. What is more, compared with a standard model, even someone who is not a Pete 379 expert will immediately see that the expression 'titanic job' is a perfect description of this Ryans truck. Although the exterior doesn't look very different from the original, the air ride, the bevelled bumpers, the bands of colour and the absence of door handles show that this is a major project that has undergone extensive modifications.

This can be seen even more vividly in the cab. Everyone knows that the interior is essential to winning trophies, so our friend opted for ostrich-skin leather and a parquet floor. You are thinking 'country style', right? In fact, Ryan is a former champion rodeo rider and with such an outstanding interior, there is no doubt he will soon have more trophies to put on his mantelpiece!

———— • ————

Imaginé par Ryan, qui est un ancien champion de rodéo, son Peterbilt d'une apparente simplicité, fourmille de détails. Si l'aspect extérieur semble d'origine, l'air ride, le pare-chocs biseauté, la suppression des poignées trahissent de profondes modifications.

C'est encore plus flagrant dans l'habitacle de style "Country" qui utilise du cuir d'autruche, des peaux de vache et un sol en parquet. Un vrai "Ranch" roulant.

*Very restrained, the old-school style strikes again.*

*The ostrich skin, leather and wood interior works particularly well.*

*American hay wagons aren't all like this, but neither are they all that different.*

## Scania 143, 'Transformers', AR Keen & Son, Harry Price (UK)

When you are the lucky owner of a Scania 143, there are two directions in which you can go. Will you stick to an old-school restoration or aim for something more contemporary, perhaps Nordic style, with aggressive accessories and a mural paint scheme? Harry Price, the owner, didn't hesitate for long. His project is contemporary and adopts a rarely seen style – few 143s have such flamboyant paint schemes composed of flashy colours and airbrushed images.

English fans of decorated trucks often choose American films for their themes. Our friend is no exception to this rule. He called in the very talented Adam Haden, the painter of great custom trucks in England, who has brilliantly depicted the blockbuster *Transformers*. The grille and the back and sides of the cab show scenes from different episodes in the saga.

Harry wanted an aggressive style, so for accessories the truck has double front bumpers, wide wheels, Nordic toolboxes, a Topline roof fairing and vertical exhaust stacks. The company name, flashing lights and the long-range lights complete the transformation of the old Griffin.

The driver's cab received full treatment too. With the doors open, the two-tone red-and-grey leather perfectly matches the exterior colours. The dashboard is also red and grey but this time painted.

Whether the chosen style is old school or contemporary, a few aficionados breathe new life into these old 143s, and that's an excellent thing!

———— • ————

Lorsque l'on restaure un Scania, deux orientations se démarquent « vielle école » ou « contemporaine » ? Harry Price, le propriétaire, n'a pas hésité longtemps. Son projet d'un style rarement utilisé arbore des teintes flashy rehaussées de décorations à l'aérographe inspirées du film "Transformers"réalisé par le très talentueux Adam Haden. Harry a su redonner vie à un de ces légendaires 143, avec des touches "customs" moderne, et c'est tant mieux !

*The accessories and paint scheme are a mix of the old, the original 143 and the recent.*

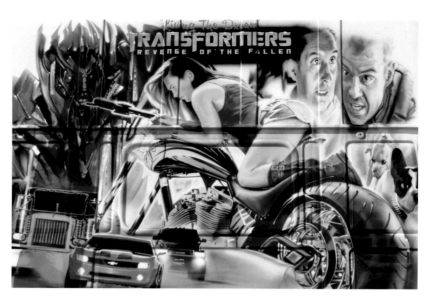

*Whether for the interior, the rear or the sides, the choice of accessories is perfect.*

*Adam Haden painted the scenes from* Transformers.

*When darkness falls, the truck's lighting works to great effect.*

## DAF XF 105 510, 'Prison Break', Weeda (Netherlands)

Have you heard of the Weeda attitude? A fleet of Dutch trucks that includes Volvos, Scanias and DAFs? These trucks are instantly recognisable thanks to the simplicity of their decorative stripes, which suit any make, and their airbrushed decorations, so dear to Dutch projects.

Before your eyes you have the latest addition to this likeable Dutch company's fleet: a DAF Super Space Cab 510 that has been given all the accessories that characterise top-class European projects.

Thus, in addition to the company's signature red-and-grey livery, this DAF has Trux bull bars, lateral boxes and side skirts, deck covers and bumpers with Norwegian-style lights and, of course, the classic air horns, sun visor and numerous clearance lights.

With this DAF, Weeda proves, if it were still necessary to do so, that you don't have to overload your truck to be different.

—— • ——

La Weeda attitude ! Qu'ils soient de marques Volvo Scania ou Daf ils sont reconnaissables entre tous, grâce à la « simplicité » de leurr décoration linéaire appropriée.

Ce Daf Super Space Cab 510, dernier arrivé dans la flotte familiale, est présenté en tenue d'apparat avec ses pare-buffles Trux, ses coffres et carénages latéraux, ses tôles de châssis et pare chocs avec feux norvégiens, sans oublier ses classiques trompes, sa visière et ses multiples feux de gabarits. Une référence reconnue !

*This DAF pays tribute to the series* Prison Break.

*Norwegian rear bumpers and wrap-around fairings – nothing more is needed.*

*The different characters are painted all round the truck.*

*The grille and the bull bars are the DAF's only large black features*

The main characters in the series.

A very Nordic-looking script.

The inverted Cs are reminiscent of the flags that floated
from the masts of Viking longships.

*Weeda's trucks grab attention at every meet.*

## Scania T580, Longthorne (UK)

For many, the conventional cab of this T-series Scania is the benchmark for European trucks. It certainly provokes strong feelings one way or another: either you love it or you hate it! Produced until 2005, these trucks are now greatly sought after by enthusiasts, and this has had a huge impact on their sale price.

When Gordon Longthorne bought this vehicle, he decided to modify the roof of the cab by replacing it with the Highline version. This was an excellent choice, as the cab is now exactly the same height as the trailer he works with every day.

In fact, Gordon uses this truck to transport gravel across Yorkshire, although it's hard to imagine this rig doing the same job as a site truck! The rear of the tractor is completely covered in chromed steel, so the smallest pebble that falls on it will be horribly noticeable – a real nightmare for the shovel driver who has to do the loading.

———— • ————

Gordon Longthorne a décidé de modifier le toit de la cabine on lui greffant la version Highline, un choix judicieux car accouplé à sa semi-remorque. La hauteur de l'ensemble est ainsi parfaitement homogène. Tout l'arrière du tracteur est recouvert de tôles chromées et c'est difficile d'imaginer qu'il effectue les mêmes activités qu'un camion de chantier !

*T-series Scanias with Highline cabs are very rare in England.*

*A superb vehicle in magnificent countryside: The Yorkshire Dales National Park.*

*The truck was created in the workshop of Ian Bone & Sons, Carlisle. The engine was painted with special paint and the valve covers have been decorated with airbrushed motifs.*

*Gordon cleans the truck one last time, knowing he will be heading back to the quarry on Monday.*

The cab's interior uses the same colours as the bodywork.

*In its 6 x 2 version, with the suspension fully lowered, the Scania has the elegance of a racing car.*

## MAN TGA Nightliner, Rubber Technology Weidmann GmbH & Co (Germany)

It is not easy to stand out at European events. There are two ways of doing so. You can either follow in the footsteps of the Scania legend, but then you have to aim very high to attract the crowds, or you can choose a less common make, such as MAN. Outside Germany, the brand with the lion is rarely seen at European competitions.

Of relatively sober appearance, this Rubber Technology MAN has all the features needed to win honours. Already a respectable length, the rig looks even better when lowered to the ground, helped by its made-to-measure skirts. This effect, so beloved of American projects, lends a radical style to any truck with full air ride. Of course, that on its own is not enough to win prizes.

Although the accessories are quite discreet, the MAN's cab sets the tone with its Trux bull bars at the bottom and XXL sun visor, neon sign, roof bars and lights up top. The cab's flanks are painted with an attractive, Nordic-style stripe pattern, which stands out wonderfully against the pure white background.

A MAN that will undoubtedly turn heads, even among fans of other makes.

———•———

D'une apparence relativement sobre, le MAN de Rubber Technology est un projet qui prend de l'ampleur une fois le camion posé au sol, grâce aux carénages sur mesure et à une attrayante décoration de style nordique qui apparaît sur les flancs de la cabine. Qu'il est compliqué de se démarquer lors de manifestations Européennes. Soit on choisi la légende Scania, mais il faudra viser très haut pour « attirer les foules », soit une marque moins répandue comme MAN ! Belle audace !

*The ground-hugging effect is an essential part of the MAN's overall allure.*

Bull bars, suicide sun visor, long-range lights and the sign are
the project's main accessories.

The blue barbs contrast perfectly with the pure white background.

*The made-to-measure skirts are the only parts of this MAN to have been airbrushed.*

## Scania CR19, 'Warrior', Renax Stängsel AB (Sweden)

Scania has designed several legendary trucks, some of which, like the company's best-selling Topline, are still being made. Others, such as the fondly remembered T series (whether in Topline guise or standard), the Streamline and the 141, are now out of production. Nevertheless, there are certain types of cab and configuration that have not been sidelined. Quite the contrary, as you can see for yourself.

Of course, the different approaches adopted by Griffin owners are influenced by the type of business they are in. As a result, it is not unusual to see very different models at European meets. One of these is the Scania CR19 owned by Fredrik Andersson of the concrete delivery company Renax, which was first seen in 2011 in Sweden.

As the enthusiast you are, you will be fully aware of Sweden's love affair with every aspect of American car and truck culture. Fredrik is no exception as, in addition to the warriors, he had magnificent blue flames painted on the body and drum of his truck. For the complementary colour, he chose silver-grey, which goes perfectly with the blue. Blue is also the colour used for the deck cover, skirts and wheels.

The array of accessories is not just a long list of additional features. Everything has been carefully thought out, like the smooth sun visor, the light bars above the cab and below the bumpers and skirts, and the chrome exhaust stacks and rear bumper. Numerous clearance lights provide the finishing touch.

Proof that, with a bit of imagination, any type of truck can be turned into a top-of-the-range project.

———— • ————

La panoplie d'accessoires du Scania CR19 de Fredrik Andersson n'est pas qu'une longue liste d'éléments posés. Tout est astucieusement pensé, comme la visière lisse, la barre haute avec phares intégrés, les barres sous le pare chocs et les carénages, par exemple. Ce véhicule orné de guerrières et de magnifiques flammes bleutées est une vraie œuvre d'art roulante. La preuve est faite qu'avec de l'imagination n'importe quel gabarit de camion peut devenir un projet haut de gamme.

*The tone-on-tone murals are beautifully painted.*

*On one side warriors, on the other side flames: a superb combination.*

*The association of chrome with the blue and metallic grey paint scheme suits this Swedish project perfectly.*

## Kenworth K100 Aerodyne, Gaël Gaillard Trucking (France)

Although for most fans of American trucks the landscape extends no further than conventional models, there is a cabover that will always be an icon on highways right across the continent. As you will have guessed, this truck is the K100.

Whether in its aerodyne version or its flatbed version, the last owners of Kenworth's 'cube' retain a great deal of nostalgia for this old Yankee box. There are very few left in the United States, as most were exported to South America, Asia and the Middle East. Nevertheless, we are delighted to see that there are still a few examples in Europe, mostly in Great Britain and France, where, thanks to pioneer Michel Gaillard, the K100 won its spurs.

Although Michel Gaillard has stopped driving, his son Gaël wanted to pay homage to his father by using an old aerodyne K for his day-to-day work. Fitted with a respectable chassis, Gaël's COE is true to the US manufacturer's tradition.

Refurbished into its original condition, the two-tone stripes cannot fail to recall the original models. French legislation imposes a certain number of rules which can limit the choice of accessories. As a result, the bumpers have been Europeanised – but they still blend perfectly into the project. Closer to the aesthetic standards of American show trucks, the exhausts are of a respectable diameter, the sun visor and front bumper hang low, the fenders have been painted and the grille has been modified.

This is the sort of nostalgic project we love.

———•———

Le Kenworth K100, le « cabover », reste la référence absolue sur les highways américains Gaël Gaillard qui a voulu rendre hommage à son père en roulant quotidiennement avec cet aérodyne.

Reconditionné dans un état d'origine et équipé d'accessoires qui respectent la législation française ainsi que certaines règles. Exemple avec le pare-chocs arrière européanisé qui se mêle parfaitement au style US du truck. Voilà un projet nostalgique comme on aime…

*US style: chrome and multi-coloured stripes.*

*These different views highlight the American old-school truck style.*

*There is chrome everywhere on Gaël's project. Note the European bumpers.*

## Scania Torpedo T164, 'I Live my Dream', Håkan Runnheden, Runeborgs Highway Star (Sweden)

Passion always inspires dreams and dreams generate ideas. Håkan Runnheden has already brought many ideas to life on the trucks he owns. One of his ideas, which has haunted him for years, almost to the point of obsession, is to bring together European modernism with the pared-down style of North America. For this, he has chosen the last conventional cab produced by Scania, the must-have of European trucks according to Håkan.

Hundreds of hours' work have gone into the truck, most notably to smooth the chassis by eliminating all the cross members and all the screw heads, taking care not to weaken the structure, as the V8 under the hood would hold its own against even the most powerful engines made in the USA. The company's colours, white and blue, have been kept but arranged in a very sober way.

As soon as the truck was ready to leave the workshop, Håkan set off for Sweden at the wheel of 'I Live my Dream', heading for the prestigious Nordic Trophy, where he scooped up one of the top prizes. A moment of great joy for him.

———•———

La passion s'accompagne toujours de rêves. Les rêves génèrent des idées, et des idées Håkan Runnheden en a déjà concrétisées beaucoup sur les camions qu'il possède. Mais celle, quasi obsessionnelle qui l'a hanté des années durant, était de jumeler le modernisme Européen avec le style épuré Américain. Un résultat surprenant qui a d'entrée séduit les juges du Nordic Trophy 2012.

*Winning a top prize at the Nordic Trophy is the ultimate accolade for many drivers.*

*The truck is very homogeneous; the curves of the rear fenders are in perfect harmony with the rounded contours of the cab.*

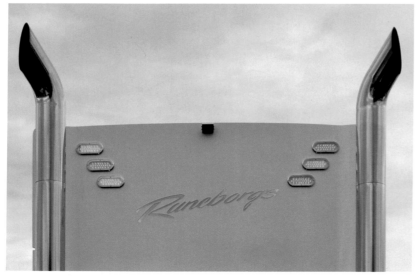

The six US-style LEDs stand proud against the smooth rear wall of the cab.

All the screws and bolts are hidden, as are the US-style fuel-tank brackets.

The fender brackets are integrated into the headlight bars and are therefore hidden.
You can't get more 'American' than that!

Seen from behind, it's difficult to imagine it's a Swedish truck.

# Peterbilt 379, 'NorCal', Ken Drake (USA)

'California only moves the best.' It has to be said there is more than a little truth in this motto. Although the Las Vegas sun naturally brings out the best in Ken Drake's 379, the modifications he has made also highlight the Peterbilt's overall allure.

Following the usual discussions at Las Vegas's Great West Truck Show in 2010, the Drakes reached an agreement with Jeff Botelho, the custom truck wizard on America's West Coast.

The truck you have before your eyes is not new, which can sometimes make the body shop's work easier; however, this 379 was in a sorry state when they got their hands on it, as it had just been dragged out of a road accident. Almost all of the truck's main components, including the hood, the cab and the sleeper, were replaced by identical parts. About the only thing to be spared was the chassis. Jeff then added skirts below the cab and the sleeper to give these areas a more ground-hugging look. Our friend then went to work on the fenders, which he changed for a more wrap-around version.

Finally, he added the accessories needed to transform the Pete from a nice truck into a true show truck, including bumpers in front of and behind the rear axles, a massive front bumper, respectable-diameter exhaust stacks and, most importantly, brake lights from a 1959 Cadillac.

Although the chassis remained black, the rest of the bodywork was painted a metallic apple green, a colour scheme that continues into the cab interior.

———•———

Acheté à l'état d'épave accidentée par le couple Drake, celui-ci s'accorde avec Jeff Botelho, sorcier du custom de la côte ouest des Etats-Unis, pour faire renaître la bête sous forme d'un "custom truck". En premier lieu la carrosserie est recouverte d'un "Apple metal" nacré jaune et bleu. Sont greffés ensuite 2 pare-chocs placés devant et derrière les ponts arrière, un massif pare-chocs avant, des échappements verticaux d'un diamètre respectable, mais surtout, de feux stop provenant d'une Cadillac de 1959. Malgré le soleil de Californie, ce camion fait pâlir d'envie bien des truckers !

*Eliminating all the handles gives the 379 much cleaner lines.*

A superb marriage of chrome and metallic green.

*A matching style was adopted for the interior: green paintwork, black leather and chrome.*

*The 1959 Cadillac brake lights are one of the keys to the project's success.*

*Sober and classic – the perfect mix. Note the rear bumper.*

## Scania R620, 'Ferrari F1', Markus Schumacher (Austria)

As discussed at the beginning of this book, custom trucks have different styles that allow their geographical origins to be identified at a glance. Having studied the earlier pages of this book, you will undoubtedly recognise the origins of this Scania R620.

With intensive use of chromed aluminium and stainless steel, and with LEDs highlighting every angle of the bodywork and cab, Markus Schumacher's truck looks more like a suit of shining armour than a Ferrari F1 car. Although the truck is from Austria, it spends its time running up and down the length of Italy.

It is a perfect ambassador for the southern European style of customising.

———— • ————

Avec une utilisation intense d'aluminium chromé, d'inox et de LED soulignant chaque angle de la carrosserie et de la cabine, le camion de Markus Schumacher, n'a pas l'allure d'une Ferrari F1 mais d'une armure rutilante de chevalier. Il est un typique ambassadeur du style « custom » des camions du sud de l'Europe.

*The entire chassis is covered in stainless steel plates, all polished to shine like mirrors.*

With its side exhausts and ultra-low front deflector, when the suspension is lowered the Scania looks like it is glued to the ground.

*Red button-back upholstery and black leather seats set the tone for the cab's interior. An LED-studded plaque spells out the name Scania Vabis, used by the company until the 1970s.*

*The windows and windscreen are completely surrounded by polished stainless steel emblazoned with laser-cut Scania logos and Markus's name.*

*There's no doubt the engine under the cab is a V8.*

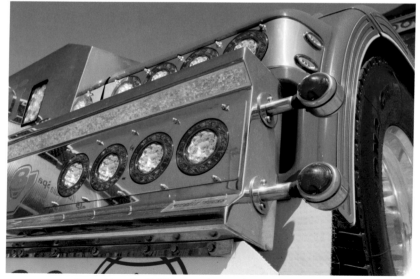

*Several hundred LEDs cover the stainless steel rear bumper.*

*The names of Schumacher and Ferrari and the red paint scheme inevitably turn the heads of Italian Ferrari fans who come across this R620 on the Autostrada del Sole.*

One of the most famous of the many annual custom truck shows is the Nog Harder, held in Lopik, Holland. Huge crowds from all over Europe come to admire more than two hundred trucks selected by the organisers.